FROGS

New and Updated

BY GAIL GIBBONS

HOLIDAY HOUSE
NEW YORK

Library of Congress has cataloged the prior edition as follows:

The Library of Congress Cataloging-in-Publication Data

Gibbons, Gail.
Frogs / by Gail Gibbons.—1st ed.
p. cm.
Summary: An introduction to frogs, discussing their tadpole beginnings, noises they
make, their hibernation, body parts, and how they differ from toads.
ISBN 0-8234-1052-8
1. Frogs—Juvenile literature. [1. Frogs.] I. Title.
QL668.E2G43   1993   93-269   CIP   AC
597.8—dc20

ISBN 978-0-8234-4834-0 (hardcover)

For Betsy and Page Burr

Special thanks to Lauren Vonnahme,
Herpetology Specialist

Special thanks also to Dr. Daniel
Bean, Chairman of Biology, St. Michael's
College, Colchester, Vermont

It is springtime at a pond.

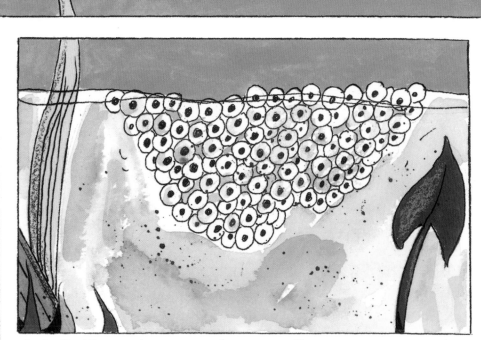

A jellylike cluster of eggs floats among the waterweeds at the pond's surface. These eggs are the beginning of . . .

FROG SPAWN

A breeze ripples the surface. The floating clump of eggs is called frog spawn. Frogs lay their eggs in water or wet places. Otherwise, the eggs could dry up and die.

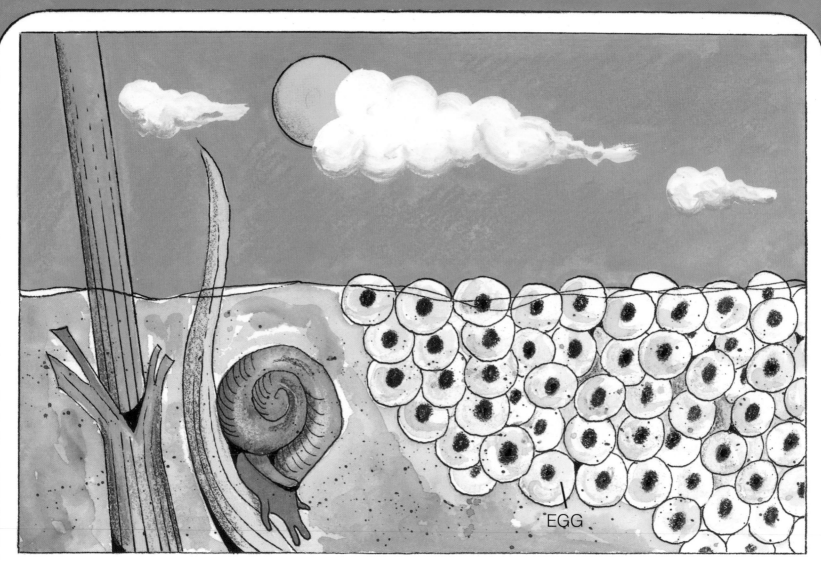

EGG

These eggs do not have hard shells. They are inside jellylike coverings. As they float, the jelly lets the sun's warmth come through to the eggs inside. Not all the eggs will survive.

Most of the time the large and slimy mass of eggs is too slippery and too big to be eaten. This is nature's way of protecting them. But some of the smaller clusters of eggs will be eaten by creatures living in or near the pond.

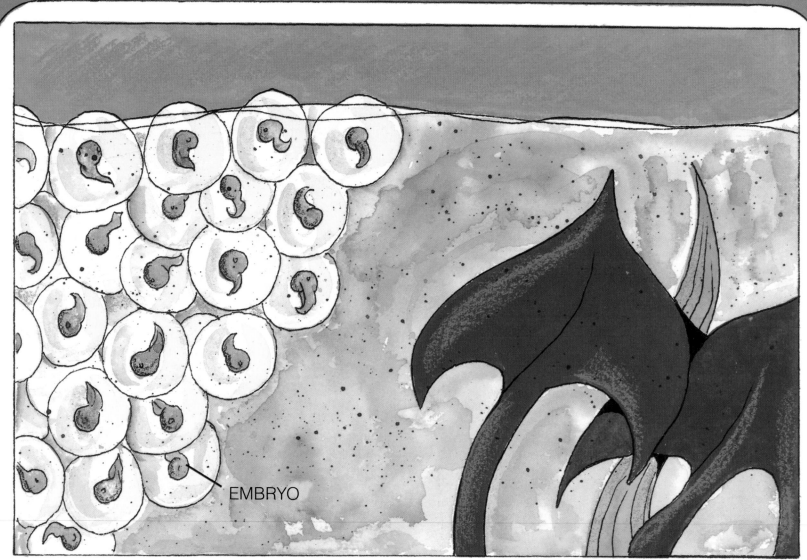

EMBRYO

The dark centers of the eggs slowly grow into frog embryos. The embryos grow until they look like small tadpoles. Tadpoles are frog babies. As they grow, they feed off their own egg yolks.

TADPOLE

The tadpoles grow until they are big enough to break free into the water. It can take from three days to three weeks for this to happen, depending on what kind of frogs they will become.

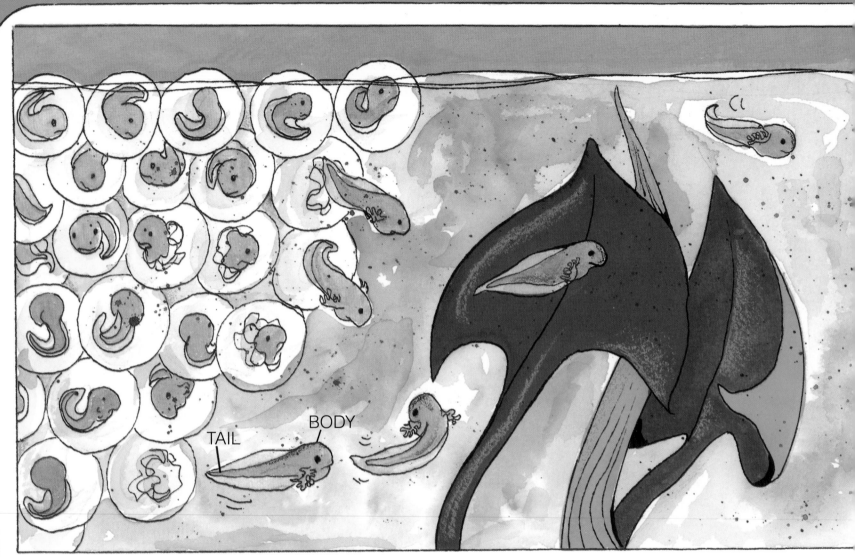

One by one the tadpoles hatch from their eggs. They each have a tail and a body. The tadpoles wiggle their tails to swim.

GILLS

ALGAE

The tadpoles breathe by getting air from the water through feathery outside gills. As they swim, they eat very small plantlike algae that stick to larger water plants.

One week later the tadpoles look different. They are bigger. Their gills begin to shrink and disappear. A flap of skin slowly grows over them. The tadpoles' mouths become hard with tiny teeth in their upper jaws.

BULGE

Now the tadpoles are one month old. New gills inside the tadpoles take oxygen from the water. Their tails are wider for stronger swimming. Something wonderful begins to happen. At the base of their tails bulges appear. This is where their hind frog legs are growing.

HIND LEGS

BULGE

At two months old the tadpoles dart about the pond as they eat. They are mostly vegetarians and eat mainly plant life. The tadpoles get bigger. Now they have hind legs. Behind their heads bulges appear where their front legs are growing.

Their tails become smaller. The tadpoles' gills inside
their bodies are gone. They have grown lungs to use
for breathing. Now and then, they wiggle to the surface
to breathe in air.

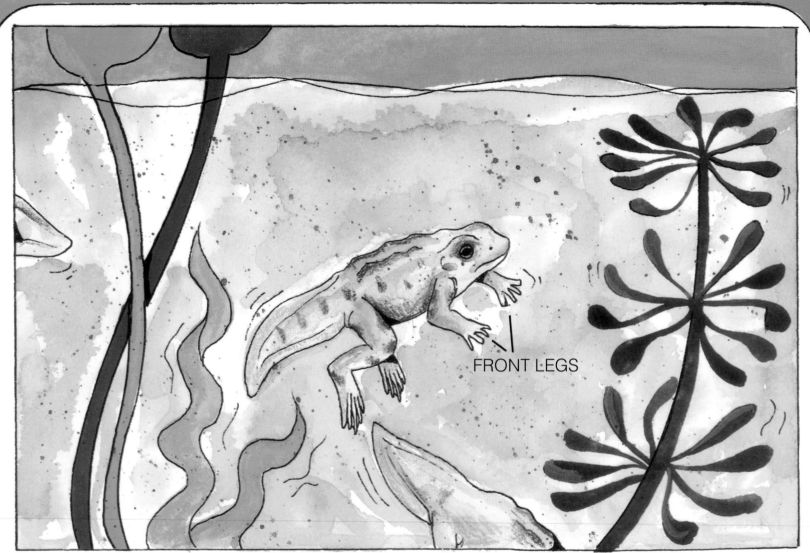

FRONT LEGS

The tadpoles are about three months old. Again, they look different. They have front legs. Their tails are even smaller. Their tadpole skin and lips are absorbed into their gut.

FROG

The tadpoles have become tiny frogs. They climb out of the pond and onto the land. Their tails will become smaller and smaller until they finally disappear. The tiny frogs begin to eat insects and worms.

AMPHIBIAN
(am • FIB • e • an)

Frogs are amphibians. The word *amphibian* comes from the Greek word that means "two lives." An amphibian can live on land and in the water.

Frogs are cold blooded. That means their inside body temperatures are about the same as the outside temperature. During the next few years, the tiny frogs will grow to be mature frogs. Then they will be able to make their own frog spawn and there will be new baby frogs.

Frogs have many body parts.

Frogs don't hunt for food. Their big eyes are on top of their heads so they can see almost all the way around. They stay very still. When something flies or crawls or swims nearby, their long, sticky tongues dart out to catch it. They swallow their food whole.

Frogs that swim use their powerful hind legs and webbed feet to push them through the water. Frogs have two sets of eyelids. One set is transparent so they can see through them. When frogs dive, they close these eyelids to protect their eyes.

On land, frogs hop about. Frogs are able to jump very far.
The tendons in their legs can stretch and recoil, like a spring.
This means most frogs can jump ten times their body length.

Frogs have enemies. Foxes, snakes, rats, birds, and other creatures eat frogs when they can catch them. A sudden leap is a quick escape from danger. For protection, some frogs have skin glands that make them taste bad or make them poisonous. Sometimes their skin color hides them from enemies. This is called camouflage.

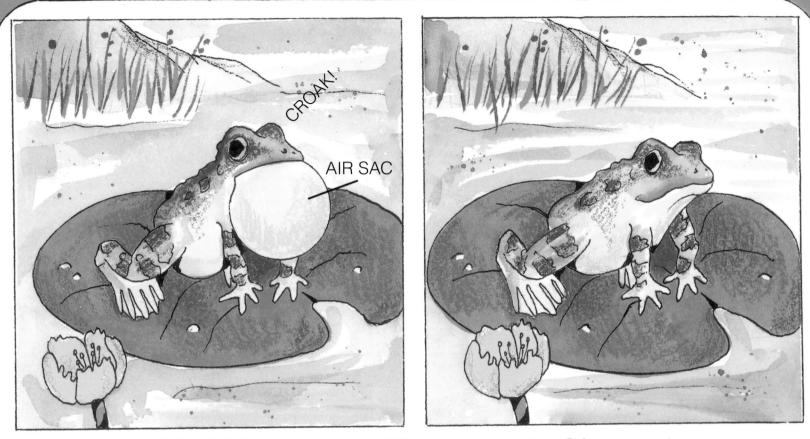

CROAK! Frogs make different sounds. Often, male frogs call their mates this way. They pull air into air sacs at their throats. The air sacs expand to look like bubbles. When frogs force the air out of their air sacs and into their lungs, the air passes over their vocal cords, which vibrate to make sounds. They make different calls that mean different things. Sometimes frogs are very loud.

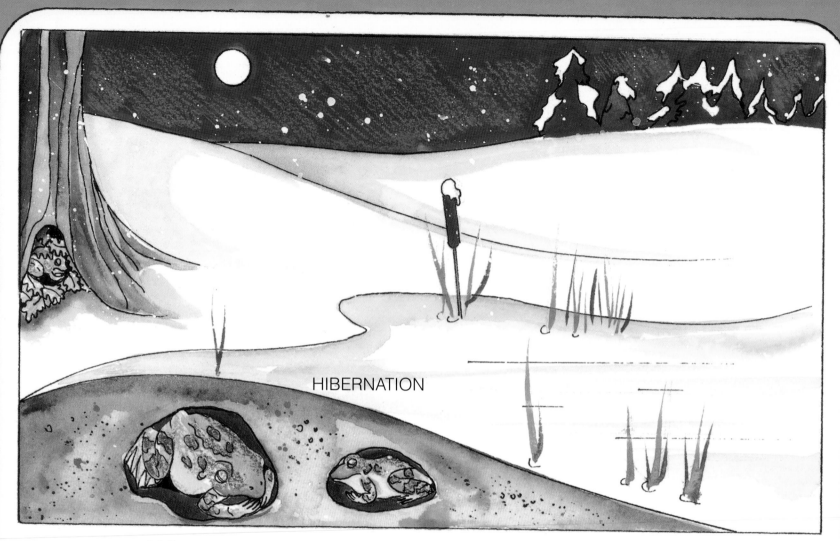

HIBERNATION

Where it is cold in the winter, frogs go into a totally motionless state, like sleeping, called hibernation. Some hibernate in sheltered hollows. Others dig into the bottom of a muddy pond or lake. They hibernate all winter long.

In the springtime, when the sun begins to warm up the ground and the pond's water, the frogs come out of hibernation. They are healthy and hungry.

HERPETOLOGIST
(her•puh•TAHL•uh•gist)

Herpetologists are people who know a lot about
frogs and other amphibians. They spend lots of time
watching and waiting to learn more about them. Experts
tell us there are about 7,200 different kinds of frogs.

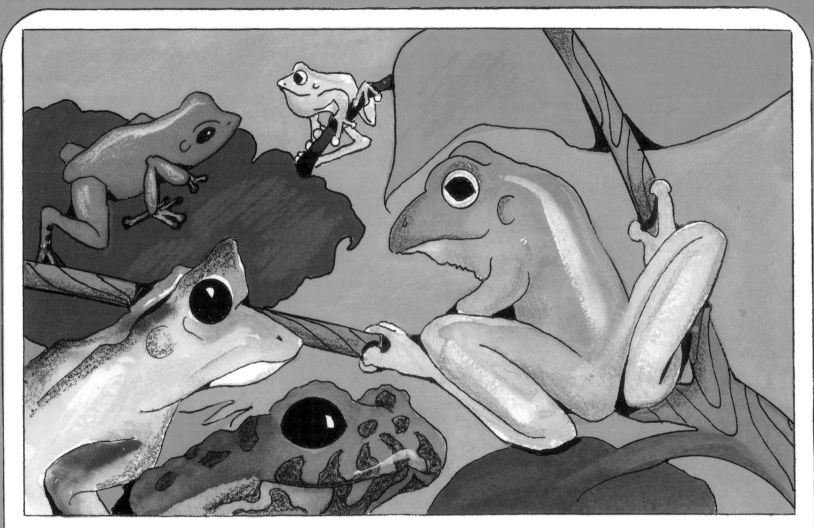

Frogs play an important role in the balance of nature. They keep insects under control by eating so many of them. Also, frogs are food for other animals. Frogs are many different sizes, shapes, and colors. It is fun to learn about them. You can be a frog expert, too!

THE DIFFERENCE BETWEEN A FROG AND A TOAD

A FROG

MOST LIVE IN OR NEAR WATER

NARROW BODY

SMALL TEETH IN UPPER JAW

LONG LEAPS

LONG HIND LEGS

SMOOTH, MOIST SOFT SKIN

CLUMPS OF EGGS IN WATER

THE DIFFERENCE BETWEEN A FROG AND A TOAD

A FROG

MOST LIVE IN OR NEAR WATER

NARROW BODY

SMALL TEETH IN UPPER JAW

LONG LEAPS

LONG HIND LEGS

SMOOTH, MOIST SOFT SKIN

CLUMPS OF EGGS IN WATER

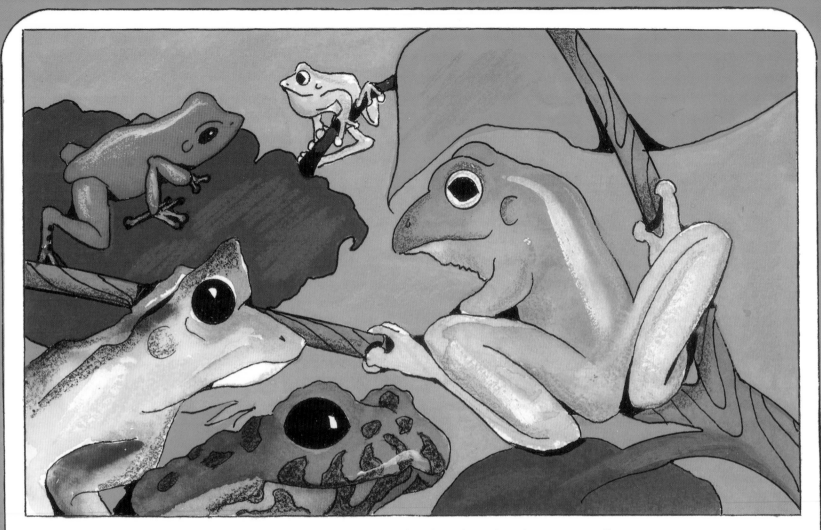

Frogs play an important role in the balance of nature. They keep insects under control by eating so many of them. Also, frogs are food for other animals. Frogs are many different sizes, shapes, and colors. It is fun to learn about them. You can be a frog expert, too!

A TOAD

LIVES ON LAND

THICK, DRY
BUMPY SKIN

PLUMP BODY

NO TEETH

SHORT LEGS

SHORT LEAPS

MOVES SLOWLY

STRINGS OF EGGS

CROAK...CROAK...CROAK...

Frogs lived at least 230 million years ago, even before dinosaurs lived on Earth.

An African bullfrog can be as big as a football.

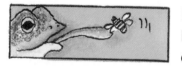

Frogs protect gardens by eating huge amounts of insects.

Frogs use their eyeballs to push down their food and help them swallow.

Each year, at the Calaveras County Fair in California, there is a frog-jumping contest. Thousands of frogs are entered. In 1865, the famous writer Mark Twain wrote a story about this event titled "The Celebrated Jumping Frog of Calaveras County."

A dwarf puddle frog is about one inch long and can eat 100 mosquitoes in one night.

Frogs have different kinds of feet. Some have sticky toes for climbing. Some have pointed toes for digging. Others have webbed feet for swimming.

Some tree frogs spend their entire lives in treetops and never come down to the ground.

The glass frog has strange skin. You can see through the skin to its insides.

Some very big frogs can eat mice and rats.

Some species of frogs are becoming extinct. One cause of frog extinction is habitat destruction. We must learn to take better care of life on our planet.

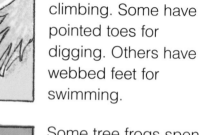